THE BACKYARD ACTIVIST™

SEE WHAT THEY ARE SAYING
ABOUT
THE BACKYARD ACTIVIST

Mark shows leadership, creativity, and hustle on and off the court.
- Joe Lacob, Owner of the World Champion Golden State Warriors

Mark is a uniquely successful leader with great tips to better the world.
- Chip Conley, Hospitality Disruptor and Bestselling Author

Mark is an unbelievable force, improving town schools, family connections, and civic sensibilities.
- Dean Warshawsky, Two-time Mayor of Los Altos Hills

Great pointers from Mark on mixing Community, Comedy, and Competition to save sea turtles.
- Rod Mast, President of Oceanic Society

Mark Breier shows us how we can think globally and act locally to improve the world.
- Tim Duane, Professor of Environmental Studies, University of California, Santa Cruz

THE BACKYARD ACTIVIST™

21 TIPS TO MOBILIZE YOUR COMMUNITY, YOUR TOWN, AND YOUR WORLD

MARK BREIER

Published by Mark Breier

Print ISBN 978-1-5499-5821-2
Kindle ASIN B07532Z7CP

Typesetting services by BOOKOW.COM

DEDICATION

This book is dedicated to the partners in all of my successful causes: Alan Bien, Craig Jones, Rod Mast, George Shillinger, Jim Spotila, Jennifer Carlstrom, and many more.

As this book explains, It **Takes two to Tango** (tip #2) and it **Takes eight to Square Dance** (tip #3) and there are hundreds who joined in efforts to connect our communities, to reform education, and to save endangered species. Thank you.

I also thank my son, Corey Breier, for managing this book project, to son Riley Breier for multimedia help, and to co-writer "Alex the Girl" Mathews and co-writer/illustrator Britt Jensen. My thanks to Lee Garverick and wife Ronda for their fantastic efforts proofreading and offering great suggestions.

My sincere thanks to the generous Kickstarter supporters who made this community effort possible:

Andy Blackburn
Catherine Boyle
Victoria Breier
Sriram Chandrasekar
Merko Dimitrijevic
Tom Engdahl
Mike Fabozzi
Steve Furney-Howe
Steve Kelem
Mike Kirk
Steve Kuptz

Dave Laukat
Jim Lussier
Bill Marken
Stan Mok
Michael Moroney
David Muller
Betsy Schmitt
ChiaLin Simmons
Alex Tatem
Bill Wagner

AUTHOR'S NOTE

This book introduces 21 activist tips in chapter two and then provides examples of those tips in practice in the next five chapters. In chapter eight, I offer "Seven Simple Things" Good for You & the Environment, a new cause I hope you will embrace. In chapter nine, I suggest other great causes to work on. And in chapter ten, I offer a call to action to improve your community.

Enjoy!

CONTENTS

Chapter 1

INTRODUCTION

I am standing in a line of 11 people to speak at the "open session" for residents at my town's monthly council meeting. I have already sat through several boring hours of official business for the town, waiting for this open session. I oppose a new town building (too tall, too expensive) proposed for construction next door to my property.

I assumed I was destined to shine when it is my turn to speak, for these reasons:

At Stanford University, I was a student leader, a Resident Assistant for two years, and event organizer. I led efforts to replace the student union, to improve student interaction, and to improve biking on campus. I was a **Student Activist**.

I went on to the Stanford Graduate School of Business and learned Negotiations (stand up on a phone call!), Strategy (always have second best alternative), and Game Theory (what would you do, if you were your opponent?) I was an **Advanced Activist**.

And then I practiced Marketing at Kraft Foods and Dreyer's /Edy's Grand Ice Cream, and as VP of Marketing at Amazon. I learned the value of leading with a single compelling selling idea, that billboards should always have less than seven words, and that if you ask Amazon users for feedback on their purchase, they will actually come back to buy another book (sorry about teaching the world that trick). I was a **Jedi Activist**.

With my background, our smallish town should be an easy win, shouldn't it? Done and done?

It is 9:42 p.m. I am speaker number eight. The preceding speakers have covered barking dogs, partying student neighbors, appeal for new drinking fountains, arguments between neighbors on trees at their borders, the need to slow cars on the street, a proposal to ban pitbull dog ownership, and an appeal for the town to reduce fossil fuel use.

When it is my turn to speak, a large digital clock turns on (we each have three minutes). I begin:

"The proposed building is over the town height limit. The town should comply with the town law. No one is above the...."

NO ONE IS PAYING ATTENTION! Council members are talking to each other, checking devices, and doodling. The people behind me in line are focused on what they are going to say and most everyone else in the audience has gone home or is taking a smoke or water break. The only one staring at me is the town clerk who controls the rapidly expiring clock.

I finish. There is no discussion. The next speaker begins with a tirade on the fire danger of exploding Eucalyptus trees. My cause is going nowhere.

Town politics was a new game and I was a **Rookie Activist.**

I need to learn the skills for **The Backyard Activist.**

Chapter 2

21 Tips for a Backyard Activist

It's been a long and winding road and along the way, I've learned that local activism is it's own learnable skill, and it's an important one. The health of our towns, schools, and neighborhoods depend solely on their citizens. People like you and me, who care, who are willing to work hard, and who are a little bit clever.

1) Pick YOUR Battle.

There are are so many possible battles, but your energy is finite and life is short. Which battles to choose?

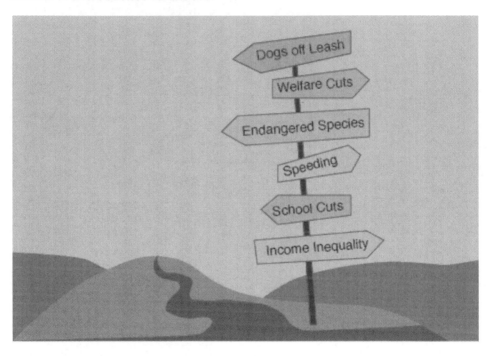

I like the adage to "Think Global, Act Local."

Pick a local battle, the one that you care about, that needs your talents, mixes you with desirable people, and offers lasting solutions.

2) Just Ask

Once you have selected your cause and identified a desired solution, you may want to "just ask" the right person for a quick solution. You may have to ask around to see who can make your dreams come true. Then just explain your problem and ask if there is an easy solution possible.

You will see in Chapter 7 that I "Just Ask" Stanford University facilities for new bike ramps, Oakland city for new streetlight, and my local town to stop early-morning commercial noise. All I needed to do was Just Ask.

3) It Takes Two to Tango.

I started each of the causes in this book with a co-founder.

This is not uncommon and parallels research of tech start-ups. Noah Wasserman from Harvard Business School finds that over 80% of tech start-ups are started by two or more people and Paul Graham, a tech investing superstar, would insist that single founders find a partner before consideration for investment.

Two people can work together to communicate the cause, to brainstorm solutions, and to identify the few right things to do. "The great thing about pairs is that they have each other's back," said Michael Malone, the Silicon Valley chronicler. "Pairs are the most stable of all teams because they are small. They are very resilient. They can move quickly."

Wasserman adds, "In general, teams should have founding capabilities that cover both their 'build' challenges and their 'sell' challenges, and it's rare that a single person is steeped in both," he said.

– goo.gl/2st22f

Consider a complementing partner to your skills. Someone to match your energy, challenge your ideas, and to offer a different skill set.

4) But it takes Eight to Square Dance.

Two people get your cause started, but there is always a team of five to eight people who quickly add strategy, technical help, publicity, outreach, legal, or operational leadership.

"Never doubt that a small group of committed people can change the world. Indeed, it is the only thing that ever has."
- Margaret Mead

In our starting battle to preserve a town school (Chapter 4), I was an evangelist, matched with an operational leader, and paired with a PR professional, lawyer, and spreadsheet master in the opening days. We added teacher experience, fundraisers, and signature-gatherers quickly to move from two people, to five to eight, to hundreds of supporters in our shared journey.

The same thing happened in starting LAH Family in Los Altos Hills, CA. This was an attempt to connect families in our sleepy town of 8,000. Three of us started it - Craig Jones, Jennifer Carlstrom, and myself. LAHF jumped out to quick success – grew to 400 members and added an annual Easter egg hunt, Halloween pumpkin carving, and a Holiday Tree lighting event to the town's calendars.

5) When There's a Riot, Lead the Parade

Often, an impassioned group will meet in opposition to a "great wrong" and come up with dozens of ideas. But, if not well managed, that can be more confusing than helpful. A neighborhood meeting on speeding cars might come up with competing ideas, such as speed bumps, or improved signage, police presence, flashing lights when speeding, or a redesign of the street. This meeting will be a riot, unless you can get out in front and lead the parade with group voting and the acceptance of a best idea.

Usea whiteboard or large paper sheet and brainstorm lots of ideas. Go through and quickly debate each idea for 30 seconds, and then each participant places 3 votes — with marker on the whiteboard or paper. Tally and celebrate your leading single solution.

6) Tell me (quickly) about your cause

"If you can't explain it simply, you don't understand it well enough"

– Albert Einstein

What is your cause, why should I care, and what do you want me to do? Your ability to quickly explain your cause – and why your audience should care – goes a long way toward success.

Girl Scouts have this campaign down. They present a fundraiser and young entrepreneur, you like cookies, and they want your financial support.

But many causes fail at their introduction to succinctly explain their cause, why anyone should care, or their proposed solution.

In the Town Hall battle (Chapter 3), I was concerned about the proposed new town building looming large over my private backyard. Few other town members cared about that, but other residents did care that it was way too expensive (a member of the next town council said it would have bankrupted the town) and that it was over the common town height limit. The building needed to be "half the cost, half the height."

Half the cost, half the height!

7) Develop an Obviously Better Plan

"Great minds discuss ideas, average minds discuss events, and little minds discuss people."
> *- Often attributed to Eleanor Roosevelt, but links back to Henry Buckle (1821–1862)*

Get ready. I think this is the single best idea in this book, is healthy for your cause, and healthy for you.

You can crow about the people, you can complain about what they did (or are about to do), but you are best off talking about ideas.

The most feared enemy of any existing plan is an Obviously Better Plan. To beat the town council's unanimous idea for a new town hall design (See Chapter 3), we come up with a "citizen's design" that was half the height, half the cost and more rural.

In a town-wide mailer that we sent out, 94% of citizens favored the citizen's design. All town design discussions then became, "do you favor the citizen's design or the council design?" and, you had to respond "citizen's design" if you wanted to be elected.

8) Just Do It

Start a petition. Or blog. Or add comments on a media website. Today. Right now.

Your energy will double with immediate action and you may find quick success.

My family – and thousands of others – got stuck for two hours on 880, a heavily used highway in Oakland, at a U2 concert and never got in. I added a comment on a local news blog that night and my words got picked up the next day in a major news edition.

U2 concert turns into nightmare for motorists stuck in traffic

By Angela Woodall
Oakland Tribune
Posted: 06/08/2011 04:47:35 PM PDT

Some fans got a taste of the real thing at Tuesday night's U2 concert at the Overstock.com Coliseum in Oakland.

Others, stuck for hours in traffic that made Interstate 880 look more like an overflow parking lot than a freeway, just got a taste of frustration.

…

"This concert was a complete fiasco and many thousands of on-time, paying attendees were not able to attend," read a typical complaint by a would-be attendee by the name of Mark Breier left on the blog of Bay Area News Group music critic Jim Harrington.

He said his family left the Peninsula at 6:15 p.m. and ended up turning around at 10:15 p.m. without ever having set foot near the Coliseum.

"Incredibly bad showing for U2 and Oakland Stadium," he wrote.

Another time, I added comments on the website from the Positive Coaching Alliance about the excessive time sink of single high school sports and how water polo twice-a-day practices (almost five hours per day) were taking over my son's life. The Wall Street Journal and Good Morning America TV picked it up.

Change.org is an excellent tool for quick action if you can easily explain your cause and proposed solution and identify a supportive base on a timely issue. See its use in the Just Ask, Chapter 9.

9) List Out Your Demands

On Oct. 31, 1517, Martin Luther nailed a list of grievances against the Catholic Church onto the door of a chapel in Wittenberg, Germany; his "Ninety-five Theses" became the catalyst for the Protestant Reformation.

Similarly, you should list out your demands when you speak to public councils. In the two to three minute allowance in which the public is invited to speak, walk boldly to the podium and state, "I have a printed copy of my remarks for the council members, the press, and members of the audience."

State your cause, why it is important, and the suggested solution. In this manner, 100% of your argument is shared with legislators, the press, and supporters, not the <1% normal take-away from speaking only.

By the way, I recommend this tactic in business settings as well and especially in medical visits with doctors. Simply draft an email with key questions, observations, and theories and print it out. (BTW, Jeff Bezos, founder/CEO, of Amazon does this) Give everyone a copy, with background, key findings, and key decisions and invite them to join as you walk through your agenda.

10) Consider a Picture to Quickly Convey Your Cause

In activism, you can combine a picture with just a few words to win the cause. In our fight to restore a town school, we wasted lots of hours of speeches before we found this picture, which best conveys that our town is vast, no longer has its four elementary schools, and the neighboring town has many schools near each other.

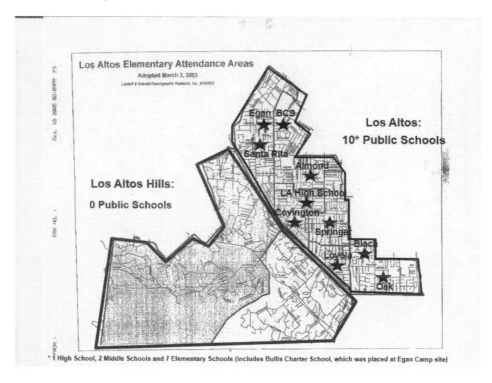

We Want a Town Elementary School

Facebook research, for example, shows 39% greater interaction when a picture is attached and that pictures trump text and video:

Not only do photo posts get more engagement than links, videos or text-based updates, they actually account for 93% of the most engaging posts on Facebook. According to Kissmetrics, photos get 53% more likes, 104% more comments and 84% more click-throughs on links than text-based posts. As previously mentioned , self-explanatory photos perform best.

- goo.gl/2JhiEp

11) Use a Symbol for your Campaign

It is no wonder that the top products have strong symbols for their brands. Think Nike swoosh or McDonalds golden arches. A symbol is a powerful representation for your cause.

In our search to restore a lost town school, we came up with a cow symbol to communicate that the district was "milking" our town because they take our taxes but don't provide a school. Read more in Chapter 4.

In our fight to save leatherback turtles (Chapter 5), McCann Advertising provided pro bono design and personality traits of turtles to come up with a central image for our campaign.

12) Develop a Slogan to Slay Your Dragon

Your enemy "dragon" is more powerful than you, better known, and has more community respect or fear.

A good slogan, like "half the height, half the cost" to fight a proposed town hall design, can slay your dragon.

Similarly, our campaign to save leatherback turtles (See The Great Turtle Race in Chapter 5) used two excellent slogans:

"Leatherback Turtles are 100 million years old. They have 10 years left."

And

"Leatherback Turtles. They are Going Faster than You Think"

In "7 Simple Things" in Chapter 8, I suggest to declare a war on plastics because

"Packaging should expire before you do."
(Plastic bottles last 450 years.)

Your creative friends can help with this, particularly if they work in sales and marketing, public relations, or advertising.

13) A Political Cartoon is Worth a Million Words

If a great picture is worth 100,000 words (tip 8), then a great political cartoon is worth a million.

Your cause needs to break through the modern-day chatter of TV/radio /internet/text messages and quickly communicate: "What is the Cause? Why Should I Care? What do you want me to do?" A good political cartoon for your cause can do this.

In urging a solution to the unnecessary car back-up at morning drop-off for nearby Pinewood School each day, I hired an artist to create this image to tell the many stories behind each day's backup:

You will see more political cartoons in You CAN Beat Town Hall (Chapter 3) and Other Great Causes (Chapter 9).

14) Act Big

It is important to your young cause to show early momentum and one of the easiest ways to do this is to take a picture of early supporters and post on social media and on your website.

It can be a candid picture of early supporters or you can stage an early picture to communicate your cause and express momentum. When we started LAH Family to connect families in Los Altos Hills, we set out to communicate participation by private and public schools as well as among different age groups, both parents and young kids, and, separately, teenagers. We put this picture on our website. In our small town, you were bound to identify with someone or some school represented in the photo.

You can also be your own media outlet. It is easy to start your own blog, build your own website, and then share easily to a half-dozen social media sites. The explosion of big media from the three largest TV networks into 10,000 blogs, social media posts, and fake news sites is in your favor. You can be the news outlet for your cause.

Politicians sense "a large and growing mob" on public issues. In our fight to save a town school (see chapter 4), a visiting councilman visited our gathering of 25 agitated parents and shared, "you really have something here. I visit with many groups on many issues in this town, and the number and passion of people in this room is impressive."

Take photos of your many supporters at every gathering. This is helpful for your website, to share with media, and to post on social media. It is also great for your victory celebration. (See tip 21)

15) Embrace Backyard Gatherings

Politicians know that ground roots success depends on lots of hosted dinners, cocktail parties, and breakfasts. Backyard activism is no different, so invite busy people for coffee or breakfast before work, on weeknights for a wine and cheese gathering before dinner, coffee and dessert after dinner, or weekend brunch.

Here's co-founder Alan Bien and I showcasing a citizen's design for town hall (see chapter 3) at a neighborhood gathering.

One of the good warm-ups for these themed gatherings is to go around the room and have people introduce themselves and explain how they feel about the cause, and what it is that they want done. In our campaign to argue for a "half the height, half the cost" design for town hall, I hosted an introductory gathering at my house. I heard amazing stories of alleged city corruption and overall arrogance by the town council and our shared passion for a citizen's movement grew.

16) Find a Funding Angel

Shopping malls of yesteryear often searched for an anchor tenant (e.g. Sears, Macys) before launching the mall. Smaller stores would follow to fill out the mall.

Similarly, you may need an 'anchor tenant' for your cause. In these chapters, you will find "anchor tenants" such as a Foundation seed grant to set up a Charter School (chapter 4) and Yahoo agreement to host The Great Turtle Race (chapter 5).

An outside party can provide needed money, credibility, or publicity to get started.

17) Use the Media to Position yourself as David, versus Goliath

Everyone favors the upstart, no-chance David versus the huge Goliath.

Position your cause with your followers and the press as the David fighting the unpopular Goliath. The media loves this kind of story.

The *Los Altos Town Crier*, a local town newspaper, ran multiple stories in our citizen's fight for a better design for our town hall. The battle of a small neighbor group against a unanimous council makes for great headlines and sells newspapers and online ads. They even ran our political cartoon for free.

A carefully planned (peaceful) protest can get things started. Notify the local media, and they will send often send photographer and story writer. Send them your pictures and political cartoons. Your campaign can quickly go local, or in modern times, spread around the world.

18) Use Sunlight to Disinfect Bad Ideas

You probably have heard the saying that "sunlight is the best disinfectant" for germs. It's also the best disinfectant for bad ideas. Activists should put their opponent's bad idea in the sunlight.

The basic concept is that you have rights as a taxpayer to the existing proposal (e.g. the proposed town hall design, the plans and supporting arguments to close your school) and you have additional rights to the public discussion about those proposals. Simply ask for it.

In the battle over the design of a new town hall, I simply asked town staff for the council's proposed design blueprints – and then took them to the town picnic and invited residents to provide their reactions. When working to save our town school, I asked through a California Public Records Request for all the emails from the school board – and then got a media double feeding frenzy when town staff turned over some uncomfortable emails (outrage #1) but then they refused to turn over other emails (outrage #2).

19) Consider Paid Professional Help

In a few causes you may benefit from legal or professional help.

We needed the help of a former California state education expert, for example, in our fight to save our town school. (Chapter 4)

A good friend runs Students Matter (studentsmatter.org/), an excellent group trying to ensure high teacher quality for all students and to reform tenure and enable merit reviews. A crack legal team was hired and they successfully argued for a California Constitutional right of every student to learn from effective teachers and have an equal opportunity to succeed in school.

Another friend, Christine Gardner, successfully stopped helicopter spraying for the Light Brown Apple Moth in 2008 in San Francisco. In the fall of 2007, California used airplanes to spray wide areas of Santa Cruz and Monterey counties, but sparked lawsuits and health complaints from residents. Christine first met with scientists from the Environmental Working Group to understand the issue, but then moved quickly with legal help to file a successful injunction to fight the imminent spraying in San Francisco and surrounding areas, citing the need for an Environmental Impact Study.

20) Build a Prototype of your Solution to Convince Everybody

When the internet was first built, an Air Force Officer built a prototype. "It was easier to show than to explain," he says.

Similarly, I obtained a quick rendering of graphic art for the Great Turtle Race from Alex Atkins, a graphic designer, to solicit Yahoo's corporate support. But the race itself featured finished artwork from a leading advertising agency (see Chapter 5).

And I hired a *quick-sketch* of a "half-the-height, half the cost" design to beat the large-budget, finished design behind the town council's design. (See chapter 3)

21) Celebrate your Journey

Activists have good days and bad days. But in long campaigns, remember to celebrate along the way. You didn't do this. A team did it and it is one of the most bonding activities in life.

"The people we surround ourselves with either raise or lower our standards. They either help us to become the-best-version-of-ourselves or encourage us to become lesser versions of ourselves. We become like our friends. No man becomes great on his own. No woman becomes great on her own. The people around them help to make them great."

– Author Mathew Kelly

Celebrate your group's 100th petition signature (Just Ask, Chapter 10), the filing (before granting) of your charter application (Save Our Town School, Chapter 4), or the successful satellite tagging of your kitchen-table sized leatherback turtles (Chapter 5).

There are few things in life more satisfying than a small team taking on a huge challenge and winning. You have abundant cause to celebrate with your new life friends.

Chapter 3

YOU CAN BEAT TOWN HALL

The best way to fight a bad idea is to develop an obviously better one.

> *- author Mark Breier*

This story leads to the #1 tip in the book. **Don't resist a bad idea. Instead, insist on an obviously better one.**

On a quiet Wednesday afternoon in 2000, the *Los Altos Town Crier* town weekly newspaper arrived by mail to my home. I opened the paper to find an article with a picture of a new town hall design. I was flabbergasted – the design was big, bold, and too modern for our quiet rural town. I immediately emailed my neighbors, who also bordered town hall property, to ask if they had heard about the plans, but no one had heard anything about a new town hall, let alone the monstrosity that was the design.

With neighbors, I set up a meeting with the town mayor. He appeared proudly, with blueprints in his arms, and spread them out on a table to share his dream. We quickly learned that the desired location was right on top of the path to a school bus stop that many children (including my

own) take to school. On top of that, it was also designed to be 38 feet tall when the town height limit for all new construction is 28 feet. We asked the mayor if the town could honor the same height limit as the many neighbors, and he responded, "We are the Town Council. We can do anything we want." We then asked him if the town would follow resident custom to "story pole" the project, that is, put up 2x4s and bright ribbons so that residents could see the profile of the new building and offer their comments. He rolled up the blueprints, said, "This meeting is over", and stormed out. Right before heading out the door he turned, silhouetted by late morning sun, and said, "The council is unanimous on this. You can't stop us."

We were stunned. We sat motionless in disbelief. The seven neighbors went through the three stages of any betrodden group: 1) disbelief – "he can't do this, can he?" ; 2) anger – he can't treat us like this!; and 3) ideas for action – we are the taxpayers, it's our town hall, and we should mobilize to stop this.

* Tip #2 It Takes Two to Tango

It was clear that we needed to have a large group of people to stand up to the city council. The group was important for both our confidence, and as a tool to make the elected officials fearful of our power. Alan Bien, a neighbor, and I emerged as the leaders of this movement. I had the vision and he had the operational skills to manage the behind-the-scenes logistics. We were a perfect pair to get things done and rally a group with the diverse skills needed to get our voices heard.

We brainstormed lots of potential next steps. We thought about campaigning by mail, public speaking at town meetings, getting the media involved, hiring lawyers, and holding constructive discussions with elected officials.

At the end of this first meeting we realized we needed to sleep on our ideas and reconvene in the morning. The next day it became clear that we needed more information about the existing plan before we could resist it in an informed manner. We realized that as taxpayers, we had the rights to the building plans, so we decided to just ask for them.

Tip 17 Use Sunlight to Disinfect Bad Ideas

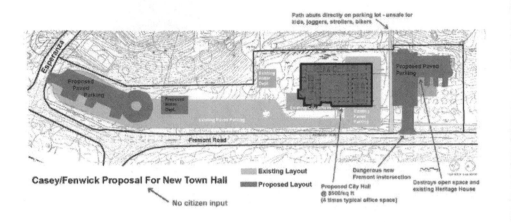

Casey/Fenwick Proposal For New Town Hall

Tip #11 Develop a Slogan to Slay your Dragon

With plans in hand, we were ready to rally a larger group. We set up a booth at the town picnic and talked to people about signing our petition for a building that would have a more fitting design and be "**half the cost, half the height.**" Within a few hours, we had 100 signatures. We were quickly turning a small riot into a large parade.

Powered by our following, I went back to the town council with a three-minute speech prepared. None of the council members paid any attention to my speech, but in this meeting, I did learn that the proposed building was $750 per square foot. I later learned that they were planning to sell town open space to pay for the $5 million building. With this new and frustrating information, the petition grew quickly to 700 signatures. I returned to the next meeting with the 700 signatures in hand, but once again, the city council didn't blink an eye at our presentation.

So, back to the drawing board, quite literally this time. Pulling inspiration from humorous political cartoons, I hired a newspaper cartoonist to draw a cartoon of the mayor and vice mayor on top of a building with cash flowing away as they terrorize families.

Tip #12 A Political Cartoon is Worth a Million Words

The local newspaper ran the picture and the number of signatures skyrocketed to 1200.

To put this in perspective, Los Altos Hills is a town of 8,000 and it only takes 800 signatures to start a recall of a town council member.

But the town council members still wouldn't stop the project and were spending $1,000,000 on design fees with a boutique SF architecture firm. As our mob of dissatisfied residents continued to grow, we rallied the PTA heads and former town officials to speak at the next series of city council meetings.

After the next meeting, the town council sent the developer over to my house to offer a compromise of moving the building slightly away from the path to the school bus stop. At this point it was too late. With 1,200 people on our team, we were not ready to compromise.

Shortly after the developer meeting, an architect friend volunteered to draw a quick alternative to the city council's design. He drew up a design that fit with the rural aesthetic, was 25 feet tall, and cost $250 per square foot compared to the city council's design that was a 38 foot tall modern Taco Bell-style monstrosity that would cost $750 per square foot.

* Tip #6 Develop an Obviously Better Idea

We printed flyers of our proposed building design next to the city council's design and sent the flyers with return postcard attached, to every address in the town, asking residents to mail the postcard back with their design preference. We compared the two designs on three objective measures: style of design, cost per square foot, and whether the design met the town height limit. Twenty-five percent of residents mailed back their preferred design (an overwhelming 10x response in direct mail), and 94% preferred the citizen's design over the city council's design.

The town council still did not give in, denounced the results, and claimed a corrupt voting process. But an election was upcoming, with three of five council seats up for grabs.

Enter a politician's worst enemy – An Obviously Better Idea. At the back-yard meetings for the next election, council candidates were asked, "do you support the citizen's design for the new town hall or the council design?" You had to support the citizen's idea for any chance to win the election! Three new council members were elected, all supporting the citizen's Idea.

Victory

After the election, I received a victory call from one of the new council members asking what I'd like to do with the new town hall design. I suggested that the council develop several different rural designs and present them to the citizens for input and vote. We had successfully resisted compromise by gaining the momentum of the crowd.

This is story of a sizeable citizen revolt and significant resistance to those in power. But nothing came of complaining. *You can't simply resist the bad idea; you have to insist on an obviously better idea.*

Chapter 4

SAVE OUR TOWN SCHOOL

Just like the alphabet, this story starts with ABC "Against Bullis Closure." Bullis Purissima Elementary School was the last remaining (of four) elementary schools in the town of Los Altos Hills. Many, many people felt this closure to be a great loss to our town. I was determined to not just mourn the loss of the school, but to do something about it.

For context, Los Altos Hills is a town of about 8,000 people that is split into two school districts and shares an elementary school district with the much larger town of Los Altos (30,000 people). At the time, there was not a single member of the school board from Los Altos Hills. The decision to close Bullis School came as a result of the Los Altos School district opening a new large elementary school, Covington, on a former middle school site. The district was proud of this new school, even building the new school district headquarters there.

To accommodate that large new school, the school district closed Bullis School, the only elementary school in Los Altos Hills. This closure was upsetting to a lot of families not only because of the longer distance to the new elementary school, but because many had just led a district fundraiser to save all schools. Bullis School had been an important linchpin in the sprawling rural town and the school site was worth a good civic fight to save.

Tip 13 Act Big

Like many issues, the impact of the school closure was difficult to quickly communicate. A picture can often help. Chris Vargas found this map and would project it at public hearings with a simple message that "this map says it all."

* Tip #9 Consider a Picture to Quickly Convey Your Cause

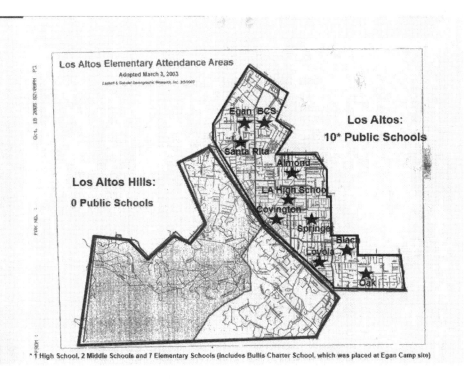

One of the early efforts was to alert the entire town of the issue and find a common symbol or logo to unite us. Jitze Couperus was a Hills activist who called out the school district for "milking our town" by taking our property taxes to fund their schools. This led Scott Vanderbilt and many others to construct large 4' x 8' plywood cows to proudly put at front of their property.

See *goo.gl/t3Mh9A* for more cow pictures.

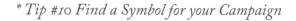

* Tip #10 Find a Symbol for your Campaign

Upon news of the school closure, a group of concerned parents gathered to discuss a flurry of thoughts on how to take action. Can we sue the school district to reverse the closure? Can we form our own school district? Can we recall the board members? Can we invite a private school to come onto the Bullis site? We quickly realized that we could throw around ideas forever, but without some school district expertise, we were never going to make impactful action.

Tip 19 Consider Professional Help

We asked the Los Altos Hills town council for $10,000 to hire a California school expert to help us and the council agreed. We hired the former head of school district assignment for all of California. We asked him the open-ended question, "What should we do?" He responded, "If I were you, I'd start a charter school."

Tip #2 It Takes Two to Tango

I became one of the key leaders along with another parent, Craig Jones. We were a perfect combination of visionary and implementer. Armed with partnership, confidence, and knowledge, we quickly harnessed our earlier frustration and rallied everyone we could to start creating a charter school. As the old saying goes, "you need a village to raise a child." Well, you also need a village to build a school that will help raise all the children. So, we got the village involved. We needed everyone from the social butterflies to the spreadsheet wizards.

*Tip #3 But It Takes Eight to Square Dance

The roles of our expanded founders team filled in quickly: Lee Garverick joined to build a school database, Acenia Farrand agreed to handle public calls/emails, Francis LaPoll formed a non-profit, Steve and Nancy Kelem collected petition signatures, Marlin Miller led teams to raise money, and Ron Haley called out unspeakable truths at public school board meetings. Dozens more joined as we moved toward the new school launch.

*Tip #15 Find a Funding Angel

Two key steps in our efforts was to hire a principal and to find funding. We found a superstar principal in Marin County, Wanny Hersey, and recruited her to join. She brought Lisa Stone, a star teacher in her district, and recruited many more. Funding success came with personal solicitations by Marlin Miller, Stan Mok, and many others, but a key moment was a $250,000 contribution from the Gordon Moore Foundation. (Often, charitable foundations can be a funding anchor to start up a cause.) With funding and staff, we were now a force to be reckoned with.

The next step was to get petitions to file for the charter school within the school district. Here we learned an important lesson: teacher unions hate charter schools. The school district officials refused to meet with us and we noticed friends who were divided on the issue. The union was telling the other district elementary school administrators that they would lose their art, PE, and teacher staffing. Not true! The truth was that per-student California dollars flow with the student to their public school, traditional or charter. The school district turned down the charter school application

To better understand the merits of a charter school, we began visiting other charter schools in the area and talking to school reform activists, including

John Doerr, of venture investing fame, and Reed Hastings from Netflix (and former head of the California State Board of Education.) Reed was incredibly friendly and very willing to talk. He told me he had "all the time in the world to talk about public education." It was empowering to have such influential people who were willing to commit their time to guide our thinking. The common message is that California schools need significant reform and that charter schools allow experimentation with benefits that are open to all.

With expert advice and a strong community, our school group appealed at the county level. The county granted the charter application and instructed the Los Altos School District that they had to provide a facility to the charter school. Despite the county's request, the Los Altos School District still refused to place the school on the closed Bullis school site and instead placed it on a shared site with one of the middle schools.

The Bullis Charter school has flourished under the Charter School Board leadership of Ken Moore, John Phelps, Wanny Hersey and others and, today, is the top elementary charter school in California and a recipient of California Distinguished School and National Blue Ribbon School awards.

In the end, our group created two great schools. In response to the start of the Bullis Charter School, The Los Altos School District opened a new *Gardner Bullis School* on the closed town site and gave us back a Los Altos Hills-based school. Both schools remain highly rated and have been key players in creating a stronger sense of community in the town.

Tip 21 Celebrate Your Journey

An extra silver lining of this experience has been the friends that came out of the struggle. Countless fundraisers, late-night meetings, long school board meetings and sheer time spent together setting up the school has bonded us together. While persevering for a cause we all believed in, we built strong social circles of life-long friends.

Chapter 5

THE GREAT TURTLE RACE

"Never underestimate the power of a small group of committed people to change the world. In fact, it is the only thing that ever has."

- Margaret Mead

The Great Turtle Race started about ten years ago. Well, actually, the Great Turtle Race started 100 million years ago, when the enormous, impressive and beautiful Leatherback turtles, who migrate every four years to Costa Rica to lay their eggs, came into existence. But our Great Turtle Race began in in 2007, when my friend George Shillinger told me that these amazing creatures may only have ten more years of existence.

George was visiting while he finished up his graduate studies at Stanford University, and I asked him what he was working on. He got out his computer and showed me seven colored dots moving off the coast of Costa Rica. George then showed me a photo of a turtle that was as large as my kitchen table.

"Those dots are Leatherback Turtles who just laid their eggs in Costa Rica. They are going to the Galapagos Islands to feed," he told me. George

was tracking the turtle migrations through a program called 'Tagging of Pacific Predators' (TOPP) to figure out where they migrated and how to more wisely plan for their conservation.

"It looks like one of those scoreboard dot races," I said.

There's something about the human psyche that really enjoys these things: you have thousands of people in a stadium, and during a break in the sports action, you throw a few colored dots on the Jumbotron and people cheer them on in a race. People love to pick a team and cheer–whether it's athletes, colored dots on a screen, or even turtles. I thought to myself that George could make a race out of this migration data.

The Great Turtle Race that developed was heralded for its use of the four Cs of great marketing: Cause, Competition, Community, and Comedy.

Start with a Cause

*Tip 2 It takes Two to Tango

George explained that the leatherback turtle mothers migrate every four years between Costa Rica and Galapagos to lay their eggs, but threats exist, from egg poaching on the beaches, gill netting (large indiscriminate nets) in harbors, and longline fishing (baited hooks every six feet, for miles) in open seas. The population of turtles was crashing. While the Costa Rican nesting turtle population once numbered over 2,000 each year, it was now down to just 50 turtles and could cease to exist altogether if we didn't do something. One hundred million years, and possibly just 10 to go, George warned.

Add some Competition

With our idea for a competition and a cause, George and I started thinking about the race idea more seriously. How would this work? This migration takes months, and I knew from my experiences in marketing that the public's time span for promotions is three to six weeks. As the idea developed, it was an interesting struggle between the scientists and environmentalists who valued science-observed truth and my marketing instincts, which favored a shorter race based on consumer understanding. We ended up condensing the data into a three-week event, but explained what we had done on the site (with other turtle science). I chose April 2007 for the race, since April is a prime month for consumer attention, unfettered by holidays and other seasonal distractions.

There was still work to do: as Atari-founder Nolan Bushnell once said, "Anyone who's had a shower has had an idea." But the world doesn't reward ideas; only action would save these turtles.

I moved our idea further by approaching a neighborhood friend who is a graphic designer with my idea and asked for a mockup. He did some great initial design for the Great Turtle Race.

Tip #20 Build a Prototype

*Tip #15 Find A Funding Professional

A few weeks later at a conference and talked to tablemate Murray Gaylord, Marketing VP at Yahoo!, and ran the idea for a Great Turtle Race by him. I showed him the graphic design drafts and he replied, "I think Yahoo would love this!"

Tip #3 But It Takes Eight To Square Dance

Add Community

Within a week, Yahoo! had agreed to host it on their website, and the community came together. I had found an anchor tenant for my cause and it was now easy to fill in others. Ten companies joined the cause as turtle sponsors, including Dreyer's Grand ice Cream, Plantronics, West Marine, each for $25,000. A four-person team of organizers formed - Jim Spotila from The Leatherback Trust , Rod Mast from Conservation International, George Shillinger representing TOPP, and myself.

Tip # 19 Consider Paid Professional Help

McCann Advertising Agency in Salt Lake City added great pro bono work and really brought the design alive. Thanks to Lori Feld Oakley, Jake Osborne, Jaime Neilsen, and many other outstanding agency personnel for their excellent work.

Find the Comedy

We assigned each turtle a character name and a fun personality. For example, the turtle sponsored by Dreyer's Ice Cream was Sundae.

We even named one Stephanie Colburtle the Turtle, after the comedian Stephen Colbert. Colbert loved it and featured Stephanie and the Great

SUNDAE

Turtle Race for a four-minute segment and two-weeks of follow-up coverage on his popular TV show *The Colbert Report*.

By the end of the 3-week Great Turtle Race, we had raised over $275,000—over $25,000 came from small individual contributions—and got at least $2 million worth of media coverage for the turtles. The Great Turtle Race and it's fundraising success were mentioned on CNN and in TIme Magazine,

THE COLBERT REPORT

and the website was frequently one of Yahoo's most-visited daily sites. We collected 43,000 email addresses from people signing up to receive daily updates about their turtle. School kids and whole classrooms took to the website and visited the science section of the website where we educated visitors about the turtles and their migration pattern.

This was record participation for Conservation International, a heavyweight in the environmental activism. All in all, we brought the attention of an estimated 90 million people worldwide to the urgency to save leatherback turtles. In the three years that followed, Conservation International and The Leatherback Trust (TLT) kept the race going.

The money has been used to improve conservation outreach, hire research assistants to track and watch over the turtles, and efforts to buy land for a park for the turtles. *And the efforts to save leatherbacks is working – the population is moving upwards toward 200 turtles each year.*

Tip # 21 Celebrate Your Journey

Months after the successful promotion, the Great Turtle Race planning team gathered for a celebratory dinner and shared animated stories of glory (what worked) and near gloom (close calls).

Recently, I ran into Barton "Buzz" Thompson, Director of the Stanford Woods Institute, and revered in the conservation field. He told me that to this day he hasn't seen a more successful conservation campaign. The important thing to remember about the Great Turtle Race is that we utilized the four C's–Cause, Competition, Community, and Comedy–to rally world attention.

Chapter 6

STOP UTILITY OVERCHARGES

---

*If you **know** the enemy and **know yourself**, you need not fear the result of a hundred battles.*

- Sun Tsu

One of the toughest battles I ever fought as an activist was with a local utility company. The struggle is an archetypal David and Goliath situation. You need the services from the company for the next month, week, day, or hour, and they are often the only provider. They're an 8,000-pound giant, and you're a consumer who needs their services: fighting a utility company is nearly impossible. You don't even have a slingshot, and the giant has a sea of lawyers.

Note: the eventual agreement, including the specific utility name and $$$ resolution, cannot be disclosed by mutual agreement. I will refer to them as Utility from here out.

My battle with this Utility started when I thought my bills were too high. I had made the effort to conserve my use, but the bills remained unusually high. For five years. But who to go to?

Tip #19 Consider Paid Professional Help

I began with customer service at the Utility but I found they did not understand the billing issues either. So I talked to a lawyer friend and **we filed a legal claim** against the Utility with the power to investigate further. But utilities have entire floors of lawyers and near-term resolution was unlikely.

Tip #5 Tell Me Quickly About Your Cause

So I **blogged to tell my story,** taking careful detail to tell the story chronologically in pictures: 1) my original high bill; 2) my conservation steps; 3) my continued high bills; and 4) my frustration, with a cartoon of me holding a "help" sign and lots of outgoing dollar bills.

Tip #16 Use the Media to Position Yourself as David Vs Goliath

I **called local media** and they were interested and made calls to the Utility, but they wanted evidence that this was a widespread problem. I suspected it was, but I had no evidence.

I decided to **send a print of my blog to the Utility CEO by Fed Ex** (As a former CEO, I always found it odd that a professional secretary screened visitors, calendar requests, and outside calls, but personally delivered the Fed Ex envelopes!)

A call from the Utility executive office came in, with "Hi, I'm Pat and I represent the CEO. Deal with me directly." But he did not agree to meet my demands for compensation.

I was frustrated and **posted my challenge on social media.** Someone quickly responded with sage advice: "Go to the regulatory association. They have websites, you file claims, and you are likely to get resolution in months, if not weeks."

Tip 8 List Your Demands

It was WAY better than that. **I filled the regulatory claim,** and got a call from Pat from the Utility the next day. "I am calling to take this issue off the table. What do you need?" I repeated my $$$ request. He said "done" and sent paperwork the next day.

I won against a large Utility! But let's review what worked among many activist steps These were the three things that helped me defeat the Goliath of the Utility company:

- **I told my story.** We're seeing the same thing happen with airlines and Twitter. A customer who thinks they've been righted will tell a couple others, a customer who thinks they've been wronged will tell thousands.

- **I asked for help on social media.** It helps you connect with other people, and those arm's length network ties can end up being key allies for your cause. Especially when your cause involves a Utility company, since everyone has to deal with them, people are aware that these things could happen to them or someone they know.

- **I filed a claim with the regulatory group.** They were able to enforce what I could not, as David battling Goliath. You've got to go to the lower authority first, but when that fails, try the governing body.

Chapter 7

JUST ASK!

The most common way people give up their power is by thinking they don't have any.

- Alice Walker (author of The Color Purple)

I offer 21 tips in this book, but **sometimes, all you have to do is just ask.** Often the recipient wants to help, or is a government employee who is required by law to help, or is at a public company and knows it is wise to help.

But I have three suggestions when you "just ask:"

- Be polite, but firm.

- Know what you are entitled to as a concerned citizen, customer, member, etc.

- Find the right person to ask. Who has the power to make your idea or cause a reality?

Stanford Bike Ramps

I learned this trick to "just ask" as an undergraduate at Stanford.

Back in the early '80s, university campuses weren't as wheelchair friendly as they are today. As I rode my bike to and from class, I was followed by an unwelcome companion. As I left each building AND TRAVELLED OFF A CURB, a constant *'thud'* followed me. The *thud* followed me across streets, as I hopped off EVERY sidewalk. The *thud* wasn't just *my* pesky follower. Friends told me tales of that constant *thud* that followed them around campus as well. It was noisy, it was uncomfortable, and, I may have been crazy, but all these curbs without ramps seemed unnecessary.

I asked around and eventually found my way to Max Mazenko, the head of campus facilities, to meet with me on this problem. I asked him, "*I may be crazy*, but is it possible to add some ramps near my dorm?" He was sympathetic and said that he had the budget to put in two or three dozen ramps, but he needed more information about the most active biking places to put them.

He pulled out a campus map and said, "Look at this huge campus and all the places I could put them." I just asked, "Can I have that map? I will sit in White Plaza at the center of campus and stop bikers and ask them where ramps are needed. We can identify the most needed ramps."

What ensued was a fun afternoon with friends, hailing bikeriders, asking if they could help us solve their problem. We provided the results back to Max Mazenko and, within a month, my dorm curb was one of 36 spots across campus where bike ramps were installed.

The bike ramps still exist, they are part of my legacy as a Stanford alumnus to this day. What worked? Three items: 1) I was polite when I asked; I didn't frame it as a complaint, but I asked–what can WE do about this; 2) I asked around and found the right person, and 3) the facilities group had money (often organizations have money; you just have to ask!).

Oakland Street Light

About a decade later, I needed yet another adjustment to infrastructure. In the early '90s, I was living in the beautiful Oakland hills. The Oakland hills have scenic panoramas, hilltop mansions, and wonderful access to the Bay Area. But crime is a regular concern.

I was fortunate to live in a peaceful cul-de-sac, so removed from the urban center that it lacked even a streetlight. One morning, as I departed for work early in the dark winter months, I caught sight of something that made the tranquil darkness appear more sinister. A beautiful Lamborghini sports car sat in front of my house, well, actually, the skeleton of a Lamborghini. Under cover of the unlit cul-de-sac, car thieves had stolen a car from somewhere in the Bay Area, parked it in my dark cul-de-sac, and stripped the Lamborghini bare: tires, rims, bumpers, radio, everything was gone. The once enviable speedster was completely stripped for its valuable parts.

I reported the crime to the Oakland Police Department, only to find that in quiet, unlit culs-de-sac such as my own, this type of stolen car strip down was commonplace. Criminals scoured the streets of the city that lacked streetlights, particularly if the night was exceptionally dark. Once the criminals found a valuable car, they drove it in and quietly stripped it for parts, making high profit for a relatively low risk crime. Upon hearing this from OPD, the thought occurred to me again:

I may be crazy…but there seems to be an obvious solution to this problem.

And again, I just asked, "Would you install a streetlight?"

I got passed along from the police department to the City of Oakland and then again to a facilities department. But, guess what? They had money for new street lights. A new streetlight was installed within a month. Flash forward to five years later, and the city passed an ordinance to require more streetlights throughout the city.

Oakland, like most municipal governments, doesn't possess the same endowment that Stanford University does. But one thing I've learned in advocating for causes that may incur a cost for the governing body is this: money is never allocated perfectly. There will always be pockets of change here and there, and it turns out that municipal governments are likely to use that cash to grease a squeaky wheel.

The other thing I've learned is that while a squeaky wheel will get greased, a screeching one gets taken off the Lamborghini. Politeness can go a long way if you're asking for a favor, as long as it's not at the expense of firmness. Know what you're entitled to as a citizen: information, input, and, sometimes, access to funds.

Stop 6:30 a.m. Town Noise

I now live next door to a town hall facility. My family has been surprised to wake up to leaf blowing and commercial trash pick-up noise. (This is commercial versus residential trash pick-up. Think of back-up beeping and the sound of a large dumpster being lifted and shaken as early as 6:30 a.m., fifty feet from your bedroom.)

This seemed odd. I'm talking about a sleepy, rural town with no commercial downtown and little noise. The city also has tight rules on commercial construction and heavy equipment operations.

How was this possible? I asked town staff members, but they did not know about this – it happened before they got to work and they were unclear if they had leverage with the outside commercial services.

So I did some internet research on the history of town noise policy and I found a noise expert. A town citizen had been influential in setting limited hours for commercial construction. He even had a mechanical noise analyzer and agreed to come one Thursday morning and measure the noise outside town hall. It violated the town noise ordinance. The contractor agreements were changed to outlaw noise before 8:00 a.m. and, after a violation a few years later, the town agreed to put up a sign on the trash dumpster affirming the policy.

Restore Laid-off School Staff

The high school my son attends recently laid off school staff in a funding crunch. But the cuts included two volunteer coordinators crucial to enlisting more than 150 parent volunteers, at near zero cost to the district, and highly valued by the parent volunteers.

My wife is both an active school volunteer and a veteran school mom – we have had three kids pass through the high school. She uniquely felt the loss of this valued coordinator.

A friend and I recommended that she use the Change.org site to mount a petition, explain the cause and get quick signatures of support. My wife spread the word to hundreds of school volunteers past and present and they used social media, email contacts, and the high school's parent Facebook page to quickly collect 225 signatures.

She presented this cause and the signatures to an impressed district school board, and the board members unanimously supported restoring the positions.

Chapter 8

7 Simple Things

In this chapter, I introduce a new activist effort. There are 7 Simple Things you can do that are Good for You, and Good for the Environment.

7 Simple Things
To Improve You **AND** The World

Swear-Off Sunday
swear off ALL disposable plastics

Meatless Monday
stop eating meat just one day a week

Trim Travel Tuesday
avoid a flight or long drive

Wellness Wednesday
improve house cleaning products at ewg.org

Thankful Thursday
share your appreciation of the world around you

Ferris Bueller Friday
work from home one day a week

Saunter Saturday
get out in nature with friends & family

© The Backyard Activist

From *The Backyard Activist*™ book | Download this PDF for free and buy the book at thebackyardactivist.com

Swear-off Sunday (swear off ALL disposable plastics)

Eliminate all disposable plastics: no plastic bottles, plastic bags, straws, dispensing cups, Starbucks lids, Amazon plastic packaging. Instead, use reusable cups and bags, and wood stirrers.

Good for you: Long term exposure to plastics can cause a number of health problems[1] including cancer, endocrine or hormone disruption, birth defects, respiratory problems, and more. Why not reduce your exposure **at least** one day a week?[2]

Good for the Environment: Disposable plastics are one of the biggest threats to our environment today: they pollute our oceans, pile up in landfills, and are even beginning to invade freshwater ecosystems.[3]

Plastic waste isn't just unsightly: the creatures that live in these ecosystems are vulnerable to the same health problems plastics create for humans![4]

We need to declare a War on Plastics. They are poisoning our bodies and our planet. Imagine any given Sunday: maybe you drink juice from a disposable plastic bottle for breakfast, then you go for a run and have water from a yet another plastic bottle, then you grab some food and it comes in a plastic bag, and then you go shopping and unwrap the latest new electronic from its plastic covering. The list of exposure goes on and on. Giving up disposable plastics entirely would be hard, but given the enormous body of scientific literature indicating how hazardous plastic is to our health, swearing off plastics each Sunday would be incredibly **good for you** .

Studies have shown that the various plastics we encounter in our daily lives can cause an entire host of health problems. Plastics have been linked to hormone disruption, causing everything from early-onset puberty to falling sperm counts and even breast cancer[5] [6]. All these problems depend on the type of plastic, but unless you are absolutely the most discerning of plastic consumers, chances are you're not sure what kind of chemical compounds are in the plastic container that holds your kale salad or organic, cold-pressed juice. With new technology, sustainable alternatives to plastic are emerging, like Ecovative packaging or Corkbrick building materials.

There are enormous environmental consequences from our human obsession with disposable plastics. Recent estimates indicate that the world buys disposable plastic bottles at a rate of 20 million **per second**. All those bottles have to go somewhere, and while many are recyclable, a great number end up in landfills, or worse, in the ocean. Plastic bottles can last 450 years– shouldn't your packaging expire before you do?! Sadly, recycling isn't really a solution – And world recycling rates are disappointing: 30% in China, 20% in Europe, and 9% in the U.S. A great deal of plastic still ends up in landfills and the ocean. Humans produce 30 million metric tons of non-degradable plastics each year. The only way to slow the build-up of waste is reduce and reuse. Even with efforts to recycle, 8.8 million tons of plastic end up in the ocean annually[8].

There is hope. California was first state to ban plastic grocery bags. Seattle and Oakland are banning plastic straws.[9] [10] [11] While there are efforts to clean up the massive amounts of trash polluting the ocean, like The Ocean Cleanup, which strives to remove the Great Garbage Patch of the Pacific, we still need to do our part[12]. According to Conservation International, reducing global plastic use is one of the keys to reducing pollution in the ocean.

No Meat Monday

Meatless Mondays:
Go meatless on Mondays.

Good for you: Research shows that a well-planned vegetarian diet can reduce your risk for certain chronic diseases, lower your BMI (body mass index), and lower your weight[1].

Good for the environment: Livestock account for over 14 percent of global greenhouse gas emissions, and experts estimate that by 2050 widespread meatless diets could reduce the food industry's emissions by up to 70 percent[2].

I know—some of us would rather die before giving up bacon, but in fact, researchers say that giving up meat products could extend life expectancies. Going vegetarian, or just reducing your meat consumption by giving it up one day a week, is **good for you.** A study of 76,000 people indicated that vegetarians were 25 percent less likely to die of heart disease[1]. Cardiac health isn't the only way that a meatless diet can benefit you: a plant-based diet can prevent and treat a myriad of chronic diseases, including cancer and type 2 diabetes. Research indicates that on average meat eaters have higher body mass indexes than vegetarians[3]. Many people report feeling more energetic and healthier after cutting meat from their diet! Finally, vegetarian diets are likely to make you live longer: one study estimates that a meatless diet could cut global mortality rates by 6-10 percent[2].

Reduced meat consumption is also **good for the environment.** Livestock account for over 14 percent of global greenhouse gas emissions, and the United States remains the largest per capita consumer of meat in the world, coming in at an estimated annual 265 pounds of meat in 2009[4][5]. One study estimates that widespread change to a plant-based diet could reduce food-related greenhouse gas emissions by anywhere from 29 to 70 percent (source PNAS). Studies show that reducing your meat consumption from a third of your diet to just a tenth could cut your personal food-related greenhouse gas emissions by at least half[6] [7]. The emissions from producing red meat and dairy products are even worse than the carbon cost of transporting veggies from another continent. Josh Katz and Jennifer Daniel wrote in the New York Times: "You're better off eating vegetables from Argentina than red meat from a local farm"[8].

Trim Travel Tuesday

Trim Travel Tuesdays:

See if you can trim one airplane flight each year– stay local or do a driving trip instead.

Good for you: Airplane travel is unhealthy. Planes spread colds, disease, and cause stress.

Good for the environment: If you're able to make sure that you travel by car rather than airplane for at least 10 percent of the year, your impact will be even more significant.[3]

Less travel can be **good for you.** Sitting in traffic and letting your blood pressure rise out of frustration is not nearly as beneficial as a bike ride or walk. More significantly, if you travel frequently by air, that can take an even more significant toll on your body. Your risk of catching a cold skyrockets on airplanes and in airports, but that's probably not surprising. The fact that airplane lavatories are a hotbed of bacteria and were responsible for the outbreak of diseases like H1N1 (swine flu) and SARS isn't shocking either. What is surprising is the capacity of other disease-causing bacteria including E. Coli and MRS (a bacteria that can cause pneumonia and sepsis) to live for up to 96 hours on airplanes[1]. Research indicates that the toll is more than just physical: constant air travel is associated with higher levels of stress and lower mental and emotional health[2]. Skipping the airport for a summer road trip can be healthier and more enjoyable. Road trips give you time to bond with your travel companions and seek the path less traveled. The flyover states have a lot more to them than just space to fly over.

Reducing your travel by car or plane is also **good for the environment.** Air travel in particular is a huge contributor to greenhouse gas emissions.

Air travel accounts for 11 percent of national transportation greenhouse gases. Though the difference in CO_2 emissions per gallon of fuel between cars and planes is nominal, the amount of fuel used just taxying on the runway is enormous. Cruising requires less fuel, so unless you're taking a very long flight, driving is more efficient concerning your carbon footprint. Perhaps even more important than the fuel emissions is the impact once the aircraft reaches altitude. Aircrafts produce vapor clouds and radiative effects[3] that add up to the climate impact being between 6 and 47 times more significant than driving.

Skip the airport for a roadtrip (or business video chat) at least ten percent of the time this year, you'll save the environment!

Wellness Wednesday

Wellness Wednesdays

Upgrade your everyday products to improve your health. Go to EWG.org to review your water, kitchen cleaners, and cooking pans.

Good for you: Your health is improved with reduced exposure to dangerous chemicals and contaminants.

Good for the environment: The environment benefits from reduced introduction of dangerous chemicals.

Is you water contaminant-free? Are the cleaning products used in the kitchen and laundry safe? Is there danger in cooking pots?

You will be surprised to find that there is little regulation – and, in some cases – *no regulation* for many of these products. You have to take in information, make your own decisions., and maybe even lead your community into action.

A helpful group is Environmental Working Group, or EWG, and their motto is "Know Your Environment. Protect Your Health." To start, go to EWG.org and test three products:

1. Your everyday water (you can simply type in your zip code.) I bet you find contaminants that you didn't know about.

2. Your kitchen cleanser: our family's "green" cleanser from major manufacturer got a "D" rating!

3. Your non-stick cookware. Read up on EWG device to skip non-stick pans to avoid the dangers of Teflon. Go cast iron instead.

Household products from cosmetics to cleaning supplies are full of chemicals we don't even realize are harming our health. Thankfully, the EWG website[4] and other internet sources[2][3] have the information we need to eradicate these harmful products from our lives.

The EWG website is ripe for backyard activism as well. The EPA has not acted yet to eliminate 20 toxic chemicals. We should all rally the EPA and our communities to regulate[1]. Rallying behind the elimination of these toxic chemicals is **good for you** and **good for the environment**.

Sources

- *goo.gl/5SNtdu*

- *goo.gl/4TT4fL*

Thankful Thursday (shout out loudly about the beautiful world around you)

Thankful Thursday

Good for you: Research indicates that the best way to improve your happiness is to outwardly express gratitude for the things that make you happy. It can improve your productivity and teamwork at work too![1] [2] [3]

Good for the environment: Your praise of the environment will join other voices, and community goodwill to set aside and preserve open space can grow[4].

Express gratitude for the beautiful world around you. Psychological research indicates that one of the most effective ways to lead a happier life is to express gratitude for the world around you. Saying thanks helps you focus on the positive things in your life, which can in turn boost your mood and **make you healthier**. Researchers at the University of Miami found in one study that people who expressed gratitude exercised more and went to the doctor less, while at the University of Pennsylvania, another study indicated that people who expressed gratitude were more motivated in their work[1] [2]. That motivation translates into a better work environment: regular expressions of gratitude can improve corporate culture by reducing aggression and burnout[3].

Send some of that happy gratitude towards mother earth, and your expressions of thanks will be **good for the environment** too. Social support for clean air, water, and land will grow. Understanding and expressing gratitude for all the wonderful things the planet provides for us and our families is an important step in protecting it[4]. Gratitude Migration[5] put together a great list of ways to express gratitude to the environment during summer vacations or other outings in nature.

Ferris Bueller Friday: Work from home one day a week

Ferris Bueller **Friday**:

See if you can pull a 'Ferris Bueller's Day Off' and work remotely one day a week.

Good for you: Your productivity may go up 13%, your company loyalty increase (resignations drop by 50%), and consumers prefer to support socially conscious businesses[1].

Good for the Environment: Commute greenhouse gas emissions go down 20% – as much as 21.6 million tons (that's about one percent of the total GHG emissions from transportation[2]).

See if you can pull a 'Ferris Bueller' and work remotely one day a week. There's a lot of obvious reasons this is **good for you:** who doesn't want to work from the comfort of their pajamas and couch? Working from home can save you the time and money of the commute. The Consumer Electronics Association found in a study that telecommuting reduces annual vehicle mileage by an average 1,400 miles per telecommuter. Think about the gas savings! If you're not sure how much your commute is costing you daily, try this nifty little calculator from Stanford: you'll be surprised![3]

Working from home is also **great for the environment:** consider that over 100 million Americans make some kind of daily commute, and the vast majority do so in cars. Among those who could work from home but don't, the US commuting workforce produces over 100 million tons of greenhouse gas emissions. Imagine if every Friday all those folks stayed home.

There are some numbers we can use to speculate about the impact of a mass work-from-home movement. Global Workforce Analytics compiled this data showing the potential impact if every commuter worked remotely half the time[4]:

- We would save $20 million on gas annually.

- We would reduce greenhouse gas emissions by 54 million tons annually (equivalent of taking 10 million cars off the road for a year).

- We would reduce our oil consumption by 640 million barrels annually ($64 billion USD).

- We would drive 119 billion less highway miles each year (think about what you would do with all the time not spent in bumper to bumper traffic!).

Friday is only 20 percent of the work week, but it's a great start!

Working from home is **good for you and good for the environment**, but did you know that it's also **good for employers?** Nicholas Bloom, a Stanford Business School professor, tracked workers at a Chinese travel agency to demonstrate just that. Between two groups of employees–one that worked from home all but one day a week and one that worked in the office full time–Bloom found the remote workers experienced a 13 percent improvement in productivity. The office work environment can itself be a distraction, the energy consumption to keep an office running is quite high, and what's more, Bloom found that workers given the option to work from home are more likely to stay with a company. resignations dropped by 50 percent at the travel agency, saving the company money with recruitment, training, and retention efforts. Remote working options are a perk, for employer and employee alike.

In a consumer-facing industry? Even better! Studies show that consumers and employees alike care about corporate responsibility. One study found that 66 percent of consumers were likely to pay more for a product that came from a socially responsible company. Another found that 56 percent of millennials were likely to leave a company if they did not feel its values and social responsibility matched their own.

Allowing employees to telecommute is a straightforward and virtually no-cost way for companies to demonstrate their commitment to the helping environment and their workers. In fact, Bloom's research suggest that companies could even *profit* from giving all employees a work from home option. Bloom's travel agency reported that it accumulated $2,000 more profit per employee it had work at home.

So, work from home on Fridays! Your boss and the environment will thank you.

Saunter Saturday (Get out in Nature)

Saunter Saturdays:

Get out in nature at least once a week–if not more!

Good for you: Even small amounts of daily exercise–as small as ten minutes of walking outdoors per day–have enormous health benefits. Getting outside every day can reduce your risk of certain diseases, improve your mental health, and depending on whether you engage in the exercise with company or alone, improve your relationships or reduce your stress levels[1].

Good for the environment: You'll help create public demand for natural spaces, and by walking outside, you're reducing emissions and energy use from driving and staying indoors with AC and electricity[2].

Get out for a walk or some other light exercise in nature! Research is piling up to show how **good for you** regular outdoor exercise is. We all know that exercise is key to a healthy life, but you may not know just how important it is:

- Even just a moderate amount of daily exercise–as little as ten minutes of daily walking–can extend your life by two years[1].

- Exercise keeps you sharp mentally, improves your short term memory, and can even reduce your risk of Alzheimer's[3].

- If you go walking with friends or family, light exercise can improve your relationships[4], but if you're seeking a little solitude, going it alone can help you cultivate creativity and de-stress[5].

- Regular exercise reduces inflammation and stress[6] [7].

These major benefits of exercise are even stronger when we practice our regime in nature. One Stanford study found that people who took 90-minute walks in nature rather than urban environments showed lower stress levels and less brain activity in the areas that are associated with mental illness[8]. Some research even indicates that being out in nature can change your brain and the way you deal with stress[1]. Getting your daily exercise done out in nature might even be easier, or at least it will seem that way! One study suggests that we perceive exercise to be less demanding when it is outdoors[2]. Near a body of water? Even better–some research indicates that the benefits of exercise outdoors are even greater when done near a body of water[9].

Getting out to exercise in nature is also **good for the environment**. Technology and overloaded work and school schedules have disconnected us from our natural world. Reconnecting with nature will increase demand for public spaces and help us understand better the importance of caring for the environment. If we understand the value of green spaces, we'll be more inclined to practice these seven simple steps, and maybe even take bigger steps, to protect them[2]!

Chapter 9

OTHER GREAT CAUSES

So now that we have covered 21 activist tips and a few sample causes, what other causes are worth championing?

I have a few. And several friends and Kickstarter supporters have some ideas. Many causes are local to California or a particular city or region, but represent common issues everywhere. I have asked all contributors my three questions: 1) quickly tell me your cause; 2) why is it important?, and 3) what do you want me to do?

And I have have added inspirational activist quotes.

All that it takes for evil to come to pass is for good people to do nothing.

- Edmund Burke

Save the planet in the next 3 years.

The World Economic Forum says that global temperatures are racing toward an irreversible threshold. Impacts will include rapid deforestation, floods from rising sea levels, and unpredictable weather shifts that could ravage agriculture and affect life on the coasts, where the vast majority of people live.

But there is hope if emissions can be permanently lowered by 2020. Plan includes six goals for 2020:

- Increase renewable energy to 30% of electricity use.

- Draft plans for cities and states to ditch fossil fuel energy by 2050, with funding of $300 billion annually.

- Ensure 15% of all new vehicles sold are electric.

- Cut net emissions from deforestation.

- Publish plan for halving emissions from deforestation well before 2050.

- Encourage the financial sector to issue more "green bonds" toward climate-mitigation efforts.

- goo.gl/dfgLz4

It does not take a majority to prevail ... but rather an irate, tireless minority, keen on setting brushfires of freedom in the minds of men.

- Samuel Adams

Support Healthy Oceans - declare war on disposable plastics.

Throwaway plastics such as plastic bags, coffee lids, and plastic straws blow into rivers and make their way to the oceans. Plastics break up into tiny pieces and are becoming part of the ocean ecosystem. Plastics have even made their way into the human body – plastics are in fish, table salt, and food.

We Support Healthy Oceans is a downloadable PDF with a public pledge to reduce all disposable plastics. The PDF is available at *www.thebackyardactivist.com*. You're encouraged to post it in your office next to the refrigerator and coffee machine.

From *The Backyard Activist™* book | Download this PDF for free and buy the book at thebackyardactivist.com

This is a clever youtube video with some decomposition facts:
- *goo.gl/Y3RznL*

Here is a helpful table that gives perspective

Time it takes for garbage to decompose in the environment:

Glass Bottle	1 million years
Plastic Beverage Bottles	450 years
Disposable Diapers	450 years
Aluminum Can	80-200 years
Foamed Plastic Cups	50 years
Tin Cans	50 years
Plastic Bag	10-20 years
Waxed Milk Carton	3 months
Apple Core	2 months
Newspaper	6 weeks
Orange or Banana Peel	2-5 weeks
Paper Towel	2-4 weeks

Information Source:
U.S. National Park Service; Mote Marine Lab, Sarasota, FL.

All for 15 minutes of human use? Really? Shouldn't our packaging decompose within our lifetime? You might think that recycling is the answer, but the facts are sobering: 30% in Europe, 20% in China, 9% in the U.S. It's paramount right now to reduce, reuse and vote in laws to phase out throwaway, ocean-clogging, forever packaging.

Organizing people centers on telling three nested narratives: the story of self, the story of us, and the story of now.
- Activist author Eric Liu

Move Starbucks and Amazon away from plastic packaging.

Here are the numbers:

"Starbuck's likely uses between **2.916** and **2.946 billion** cups at their stores, or an average of **8,070,428** per day. Interestingly, Starbucks' own website states that they 'account for approximately **4 billion** cups globally each year.'"
- goo.gl/nKWwTY

"Amazon ships an average of **608 million** packages each year, which equates to (an estimated) **1,600,000** packages a day. "That's a lot of plastic inserts."
- goo.gl/1CqUjv

As a frequent Starbucks patron, I switched to a reusable plastic cup. I was saddened to learn that Starbucks' own reusable goal as a corporation was 25% by 2015 but they have achieved less than two percent.

Let's put pressure on these market leaders to join our movement to reduce all disposable plastics.

Do not go where the path may lead, go instead where there is no path and leave a trail.
- Ralph Waldo Emerson

"Half the time, half the travel" for professionalized Kid Sports

The concentration on school and club sports is increasingly taking over hours and hours of children's lives and crowding out family time, personal development, and exposure to other activities and hobbies. Team sports also add to global warming through unnecessarily long drives and plane trips to tournaments and away games

I hired an artist to develop this illustration that shows how time spent playing youth sports can be "out of their life swim lanes" and crowds out other healthy elements of a young life.

Kid Sports violates "swim lanes" of life.

© Mark Breier

Let's make reasonable limits on sports time per day (e.g. under two hours) and encourage freedom for our kids to pursue multiple sports and hobbies, and limit the travel to a 20-mile radius, with exceptions for end of year tournaments. Play your local teams twice, for example.

Be who you are and say what you feel, because those who mind don't matter, and those who matter don't mind.

– Bernard M. Baruch

Support Global Goals to reduce poverty, inequality, and climate change

In September 2015, 193 world leaders agreed to 17 **Global Goals for Sustainable Development**. If these **Goals** are completed, it would mean an end to extreme poverty, inequality and climate change by 2030.

The goals are inspiring and each have an "act local" component for you to champion as you "think global." See more at: www.globalgoals.org

Action is the antidote to despair.

– Joan Baez

Support Sunlight on Local Government

As tip 17 suggests, "use sunlight to disinfect bad ideas." There is a group dedicated to this cause.

The Sunlight Foundation is a national, nonpartisan, nonprofit organization that wants to make government and politics more accountable and transparent to all. Their overarching goal is to achieve changes in the law to require real-time, online transparency for all government information. The Foundation began in 2006 with a focus on the U.S. Congress, but their open government work now takes place at local, state, federal, and international fronts.

- goo.gl/QNY1Mi

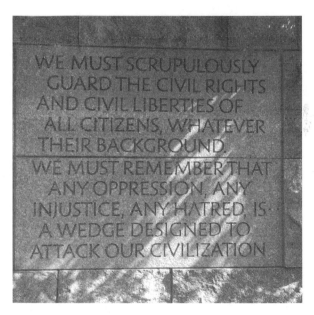

From the Franklin Delano Roosevelt Memorial

Save Bees

Andy Drexler and Blondie's Deborah Harry encourage us to save the world's bee population.

The simple argument is that bees are directly responsible for much of the world's food production, that they are disappearing in droves, and that we need to pursue organic farming and quickly investigate suspected pesticides.

Wikipedia resources show that global crops with honey bee pollination was estimated at close to $200 billion in 2005 and the collapse of bee populations is estimated to raise farming costs 20%. One of the leading suspects is neonicotinoid, a common ingredient in pesticides. Europe restricted use of this ingredient in 2013.

The future is already here, but it's just not very evenly distributed.

- William Gibson

Lower Greenhouse Emissions

If we can decrease gas emissions , we can have healthier air and decrease the warming of the atmosphere which is causing ice caps to melt, sea levels to rise, and weather to change.

A few people have resources to buy an electric vehicle, but one of the easiest ways for everybody is to lease one – lowest up to the minute lease prices can be found at:

- goo.gl/PszVyt

Another way to help is to become a member or donate to leading organizations on this issue. Top ones include:

Environment California www.environmentcalifornia.org

Environmental Defense Fund www.edf.org

Natural Resource Defense Council www.nrdc.org/

People are very frightened and feel really doomed in America these days, and I just wanted to help people get their sense of humor about it and to realize how much isn't a problem. If you take an action, take a really healthy or loving or friendly action, you'll have loving and friendly feelings.

- author Annie Lamott

Support Independent, Nonprofit News

The world needs an unbiased, non-profit news organization that performs in-depth investigation of current news items regarding politics, threats to democracy, big money, and the environment. The entity needs to be free from corporate and government biases.

Steve Kelem, a Kickstarter supporter, recommends WhoWhatWhy.org, and asks that donors contribute and help get the word out.

Don't let complexity stop you. Be activists. Take on the big inequities. It will be one of the great experiences of your life.

- Bill Gates

Reform U.S. Prison Approach

In October 2013, the **incarceration** rate of the United States of America was the highest in the world, at 716 **per** 100,000 of the **national** population. While the United States represents about 4.4 percent of the world's population, it houses around 22 percent of the world's **prisoners**.

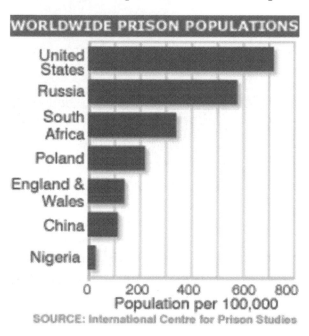

What gives? The unsuccessful war on drugs is one major influencer. The Washington Post reports, American "police make more arrests for marijuana possession alone than for all violent crimes combined."
- *goo.gl/i7Adp7*

And there are other issues:

Prisons are crazy expensive: In California, the Los Angeles Times reports that the cost to incarcerate one prisoner for one year costs over $75,000 and exceeds the tuition for one year at Harvard.
- *goo.gl/FZ9QkU*

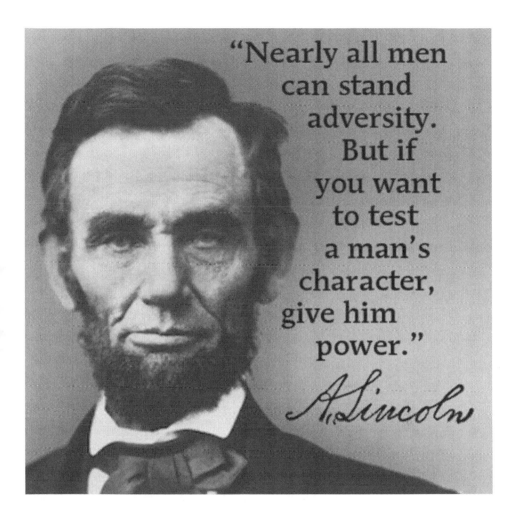

"Nearly all men can stand adversity. But if you want to test a man's character, give him power."

A. Lincoln

Stop Police Brutality

We have all witnessed widespread police brutality in our lifetimes, from college football game sheriff roughly handling the drunk and disorderly to TV news broadcasting showing the kicking or beating of suspects. I have even had a first-person experience with a mall cop beating up my sister. Clearly there is some combination of on-police cameras, conflict resolution classes, and training of alternative methods that can help the situation.

But the police killing of black people, with virtually no accountability, deserves special call-out. This website does excellent job of summarizing real-time regional data on deaths and the appalling lack of police convictions.

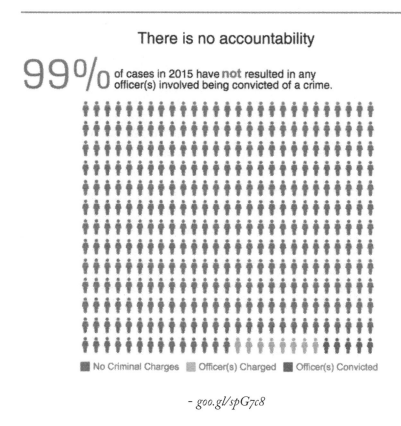

There is no accountability

99% of cases in 2015 have not resulted in any officer(s) involved being convicted of a crime.

■ No Criminal Charges ■ Officer(s) Charged ■ Officer(s) Convicted

- goo.gl/spG7c8

How wonderful it is that nobody need wait a single moment before starting to improve the world.

– Anne Frank

Just the Facts

Former Microsoft CEO Steve Ballmer observes that we are living in a world of increasingly debatable truths and questionable facts and he invested $10 million to start USAFACTS.org, a website which aggregates the statistics behind the missions of the U.S. Government.

For example, here's how the U.S. is doing versus four of our own Constitution's mandates:

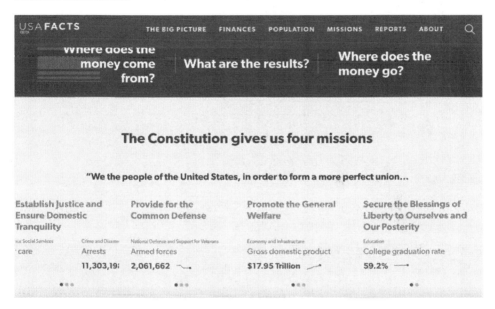

See more at usafacts.org

You do it for yourself. You don't expect to change the world. You don't even expect to influence your family or your friends. You do it because you can't not do it and be who you are. Or who you're meant to be.

- Martin Sheen

Support smart land-use policies

Promote sound land use policies that better a community – its long-term economic vitality, high agricultural productivity, environmental health, and social equity.

Mike Delapa runs LandWatch Monterey County. By encouraging greater public participation in planning, LandWatch shows how to connect people to government, address human needs and inspire conservation of natural resources.

You can donate at *goo.gl/icUK3b*

Unless someone like you cares a whole awful lot,
Nothing is going to get better. It's not.
– Dr. Seuss, the Lorax

Support Venture Investment in Women

In 2016, women received less than five percent of all venture investment and three percent of all venture capital funding to launch startup businesses despite the fact that women spend 80% of consumer spending. While women represent one of the largest segments of new small business owners in the US, funding has not kept up with this change.

Research shows that women-led companies have a higher return on investment for investors than male-led companies. Consider joining the Binders Project (www.bindersproject.com) and join women founders and funders to help change the ratio of investments and help invest in women-founded startups.

It had long since come to my attention that people of accomplishment rarely sat back and let things happen to them. They went out and happened to things.

– Leonardo Da Vinci

Help Children and Families in Life Threatening Conditions

Make-A-Wish Southern Florida grants wishes to children battling life threatening conditions and their families.

Because there is nothing better than a child's joy to brighten the world.

People can help. Donate: - *goo.gl/xLWZvT*

You never change things by fighting the existing reality.
To change something, build a new model that makes the existing model obsolete.

– R. Buckminster Fuller

—

Support Healthy Coral Reefs

Coral Reef Alliance (CORAL.org), a nonprofit devoted to coral reef conservation.

Reefs are important and in danger:

1. 25% of all marine life depends on coral reefs

2. 275M people depend on coral reefs for food and income

3. 27% of the world's reefs have already been lost, and the rest are threatened

4. $375B per year in food and tourism is in jeopardy

Support CORAL.org and other organizations working with communities around the globe to improve local conditions on reefs such as: reduce overfishing, create and enforce marine protected areas, improve wastewater systems, reduce agricultural runoff, while at same time supporting research and implementation of programs to foster spread of heat and climate resistant species of coral, so reefs can adapt and thrive in the face of climate change.

Dripping water hollows out stone, not through force but through persistence.

- Ovid

Improve Non-Profit Efficiency

Make non-profits succeed by helping them to operate simply. Many non-profits struggle to make their ends meet. Often, their resources are not optimally utilized.

Use a proven business operational framework to manage your journey to success at profit-circles.com/start

---

Get up, stand up, Stand up for your rights. Get up, stand up, Don't give up the fight.

- Bob Marley

Insist on Educational Excellence for all

We are a countywide partnership of school districts, community members, nonprofit directors, government officials, neighborhood leaders, post-secondary educators, CEOs and funders, working together to make educational excellence a reality for all students in Marin, regardless of their race or family income.

- goo.gl/bkBzHa

No one's gonna take me alive
The time has come to make things right
You and I must fight for our rights
You and I must fight to survive

- Muse, Knights of Cydonia

Ensure Affordable Housing for All

Many communities are challenged by affordable family housing, senior housing, veterans housing, special needs and transitional housing addressing homelessness, mental illness, and addiction recovery.

Wakeland Housing and Development Company address the significant affordable housing problems here in San Diego and is the second largest affordable housing provider in San Diego County.

With over 5,000 units now in their portfolio, each of their communities integrate a strong social service component on site, as well as through strategic community partnerships to address the specific critical needs of our residents.

Wakeland would love people to support affordable housing efforts in other communities and appreciate donations to Wakeland Housing and Development Company 1230 Columbia St, suite 950, San Diego, CA 92101.

- goo.gl/5ejtvs

Our soul longs to be of service in some way. It's why we are here. If you weren't meant to touch the world in some way, you wouldn't be here.

What act of service calls to you? Even the smallest thing has an effect in eternity.

- Eileen Anglin

Chapter 10

A CALL TO ACTION

Towns are largely run by volunteers.

Everything special about your town, schools, and local life is not a given. A healthy town can stay that way, or not. A troubled town can stay that way, or not.

We live in places of constant change with many forces in play. Some forces can be corrupting - greed, vanity, and power- among many others. But civic power to improve your town, your community, your world is the greatest force.

You are hereby empowered, with these 21 tips, to make the changes that matter in your world. You'll figure it out as you go, scrape together enough free time in a busy life, gather enough courage to speak out or call that meeting.

But who better than you to care, and to take action?

What will you do with this power?

Chapter 11

7 Simple Things Bibliography

Swear Off Sunday

1. Ecology Center. "Adverse Health Effects of Plastic." Ecology Center, Ecology Center, *goo.gl/Ldpgi8*.

2. Centers for Disease Control and Prevention. "National Report on Human Exposure to Environmental Chemicals." Centers for Disease Control and Prevention, Centers for Disease Control and Prevention, 14 Apr. 2017, *goo.gl/iThN64*.

3. Schlossberg, Tatiana. "The Immense, Eternal Footprint Humanity Leaves on Earth: Plastics." The New York Times, The New York Times, 19 July 2017, *goo.gl/QNVKJX*.

4. Bergen, Molly. "Reducing Global Plastic Use Is Key to Fight Ocean Pollution". Human Nature – Conservation International Blog, Conservation International, 16 July 2013, *goo.gl/MJCdbr*.

5. "Exposure to Chemicals in Plastic." Breastcancer.org, Breastcancer. org, 2017, *goo.gl/xvnGfN*.

6. Ghosh, Pallab. "Sperm Count Drop 'Could Make Humans Extinct'." BBC News, BBC, 25 July 2017, www.bbc.com/news/health-40719743.

7. Mauney, Laura. "The 30% Solution - Why Recycling Works but Doesn't Work." Danimer Scientific, Danimer Scientific The Biopolymer Company, 6 July 2016, *goo.gl/KJwvne*.

8. Rogers, Paul. "Plastic to Be Phased out at Major American Aquariums." The Mercury News, The Mercury News, 10 July 2017, *goo.gl/78qgiH*.

9. Fimrite, Peter. "Plastic Straws Stir up Environmental Debate in Berkeley." San Francisco Chronicle, SFGate, 2 June 2017, *goo.gl/zxwxoe*.

10. "McDonald's Has a 3.5 Million per Day Plastic Straw Habit..." SumOfUs, *goo.gl/ZyU45D*.

11. Densham, Ariana. "The Final Straw?" Greenpeace, Greenpeace UK, 27 July 2017, www.greenpeace.org.uk/final-straw-20170310/.

12. Linnenkoper, Kirstin. "How We Can Eliminate 50% of Ocean Plastics by 2022." Recycling International, Recycling International, July 2017,

Meatless Monday

1. "Becoming a Vegetarian." Harvard Women's Health Watch, Harvard Medical School, 18 Mar. 2016, *goo.gl/755nE7*.

2. Springmann, Marco, et al. "Analysis and Valuation of the Health and Climate Change Cobenefits of Dietary Change." Proceedings of the National Academy of Sciences, vol. 113, no. 15, 2016, pp. 4146–4151., doi:10.1073/pnas.1523119113.

3. Rizzo, Nico S., et al. "Nutrient Profiles of Vegetarian and Nonvegetarian Dietary Patterns." Journal of the Academy of Nutrition and Dietetics, vol. 113, no. 12, 2013, pp. 1610–1619., doi:10.1016/j.jand.2013.06.349.

4. Gerber, P.J., Steinfeld, H., Henderson, B., Mottet, A., Opio, C., Dijkman, J., Falcucci, A. & Tempio, G. 2013. Tackling climate change through livestock – A global assessment of emissions and mitigation opportunities. Food and Agriculture Organization of the United Nations (FAO), Rome. www.fao.org/3/i3437e.pdf.

5. "List of Countries by Meat Consumption." Wikipedia, Wikimedia Foundation, 16 Aug. 2017, *goo.gl/u2iB6r*.

6. Column 5. "Big Facts on Climate Change, Agriculture and Food Security." CGIAR Big Facts, CCAFS, CGIAR, *goo.gl/xkBFCZ*.

7. Pradhan, Prajal, et al. "Embodied Greenhouse Gas Emissions in Diets." PLoS ONE, vol. 8, no. 5, 2013, doi:10.1371/journal.pone.0062228.

8. Katz, Josh, and Jennifer Daniel. "What You Can Do About Climate Change." The New York Times, The New York Times, 2 Dec. 2015, *goo.gl/294Fz7*.

Trim Travel Tuesday

1. Kim, Soo. "What Happens to Your Body on a Flight." The Telegraph, Telegraph Media Group, 6 May 2016, *goo.gl/4zjukF*.

2. Cohen, Scott A, and Stefan Gössling. "A Darker Side of Hypermobility." Environment and Planning A, vol. 47, no. 8, 2015, pp. 166–1679., doi:10.1177/0308518x15597124.

3. Wihbey, John. "Evolving Climate Math of Flying vs. Driving " Yale Climate Connections, The Yale Center for Environmental Communication, 15 Sept. 2015, *goo.gl/whk8Pu*.

Wellness Wednesday

1. Walker, Bill, and Melanie Benesh. "Under New Safety Law, 20 Toxic Chemicals EPA Should Act On Now." EWG, Environmental Working Group, 21 July 2016, *goo.gl/Cm9xRV*.

2. Gardner, Christine. "Product Resources." More Green Moms, Sept. 2009, www.moregreenmoms.com/product_resources/.

3. Gardner, Christine. "Online Resources." More Green Moms, 27 Jan. 2008, www.moregreenmoms.com/product_resources/.

4. Environmental Working Group. "EWG VERIFIED™ Takes Aim At Toxic Ingredients In Consumer Products." EWG Verified™, Environmental Working Group, www.ewg.org/ewgverified/.

Thankful Thursday

1. Greenberg, Melanie. "How Gratitude Leads to a Happier Life." Psychology Today, Sussex Publishers, 22 Nov. 2015, *goo.gl/x8VaA4*.

2. Harvard Medical School. "Giving Thanks Can Make You Happier." Healthbeat, Harvard Health Publications, *goo.gl/TxU3G9*.

3. Vozza, Stephanie. "The Science Of Gratitude And Why It's Important In Your Workplace." Fast Company, Fast Company, 23 Nov. 2016, *goo.gl/RQ87DL*.

4. PBS. "Gratitude and the Environment." PBS LearningMedia, PBS, *goo.gl/P5fx91*.

5. Gratitude Migration. "5 Ways to Show Your Gratitude to the Environment." GRATITUDE MIGRATION, *goo.gl/Bh6qMm*.

Ferris Bueller Friday

1. Bloom, Nicholas, et al. "Does Working from Home Work? Evidence from a Chinese Experiment *." The Quarterly Journal of Economics, vol. 130, no. 1, 2014, pp. 165–218., doi:10.1093/qje/qju032.

2. Environmental Protection Agency. "Sources of Greenhouse Gas Emissions." EPA, Environmental Protection Agency, 14 Apr. 2017, *goo. gl/7EfaC2*.

3. "Commute Cost & Carbon Emissions Calculator." Stanford Parking & Transportation Services, Stanford University, *goo.gl/eqxqeH*.

4. Perez, Maria. "Infographic: Can Remote Work Help the Environment?." WebEx Blog, Cisco, *goo.gl/igmykS*.

Saunter Saturday

1. Reynolds, Gretchen. "Can Housework Help You Live Longer?" The New York Times, The New York Times, 14 Nov. 2012, *goo.gl/LUfFky*

2. Gladwell, Valerie F, et al. "The Great Outdoors: How a Green Exercise Environment Can Benefit All." Extreme Physiology & Medicine, vol. 2, no. 1, 2013, p. 3., doi:10.1186/2046-7648-2-3.

3. Godman, Heidi. "Regular Exercise Changes the Brain to Improve Memory, Thinking Skills." Harvard Health Blog, 29 Nov. 2016, *goo.gl/Fg5q3K*.

4. Robbins, Sarah J. "5 Questions That'll Bring You Closer to Your Dad." MSN, 25 May 2017, *goo.gl/73WFja*.

5. Marz, Justin Talbot-ZornLeigh, et al. "The Busier You Are, the More You Need Quiet Time." Harvard Business Review, 17 Mar. 2017, *goo.gl/a4AkLS*.

6. Mayo Clinic. "Exercise and Stress: Get Moving to Manage Stress." Mayo Clinic, Mayo Foundation for Medical Education and Research, 16 Apr. 2015, *goo.gl/e2P82S*.

7. Woods, Jeffrey A. et al. "Exercise, Inflammation and Aging." Aging and Disease 3.1 (2012): 130–140. *goo.gl/4yPWj8*.

8. Bratman, Gregory N., et al. "Nature Experience Reduces Rumination and Subgenual Prefrontal Cortex Activation." Proceedings of the National Academy of Sciences, vol. 112, no. 28, 2015, pp. 8567–8572., doi:10.1073/pnas.1510459112.

9. Hackspirit. "A Scientist Reveals What Being near the Ocean Actually Does to Your Brain." Hack Spirit, 5 Aug. 2017, *goo.gl/6uxJk3*.

About the Author

Mark Breier is an author, speaker, and tech investor.

His work experience includes executive positions with consumer companies such as Kraft Foods, and Dreyer's/Edy's Grand Ice Cream and at tech leaders such as VP of Marketing at Amazon.com, CEO of Beyond.com, and CMO at Plantronics. He currently is a Venture Partner with IQT, investing in tech start-ups for the U.S. Intelligence Community.

Mark is married, has 3 boys, and lives in Silicon Valley. He enjoys weekly basketball, pool basketball, and street hockey and enjoys bi-monthly poker games. Mark enjoys gardening, including growing big pumpkins.

This is Mark's 3rd book. Prior books include: The 10-Second Internet Manager (Crown Books 2001) encouraged workers to "act fast, act smart." Life is a Game *Group Games for Kids, Teens, and Adults* came out in 2013.

Made in the USA
Middletown, DE
27 April 2018